When I Was
Little

Paul Humphrey

Photography by Chris Fairclough

W
FRANKLIN WATTS
LONDON•SYDNEY

First published in 2005 by
Franklin Watts
96 Leonard Street
London EC2A 4XD

Franklin Watts Australia
Level 17/207 Kent Street
Sydney NSW 2000

ISBN 0 7496 6174 7 (hbk)
ISBN 0 7496 6186 0 (pbk)

Dewey classification number 305.232

A CIP catalogue record for this book is available
from the British Library.

Planning and production by Discovery Books Limited
Editor: Rachel Tisdale
Designer: Ian Winton
Photography: Chris Fairclough
Series advisors: Diana Bentley MA and Dee Reid MA,
Fellows of Oxford Brookes University

The author, packager and publisher would like to thank the
following people for their participation in this book: Sam, Oliver,
Tim and Jane Yarnold; Alfie and Caroline Mann.

Printed in China

Contents

I am a big boy now ...

... but once I was
a little baby.

When I
was a baby,
my mum
fed me.

I played
on my
play mat.

I had to wear a nappy.

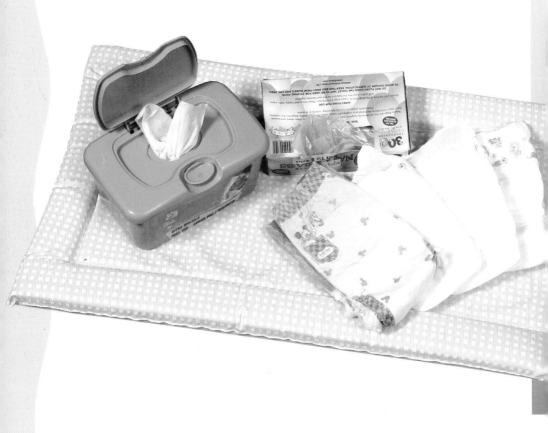

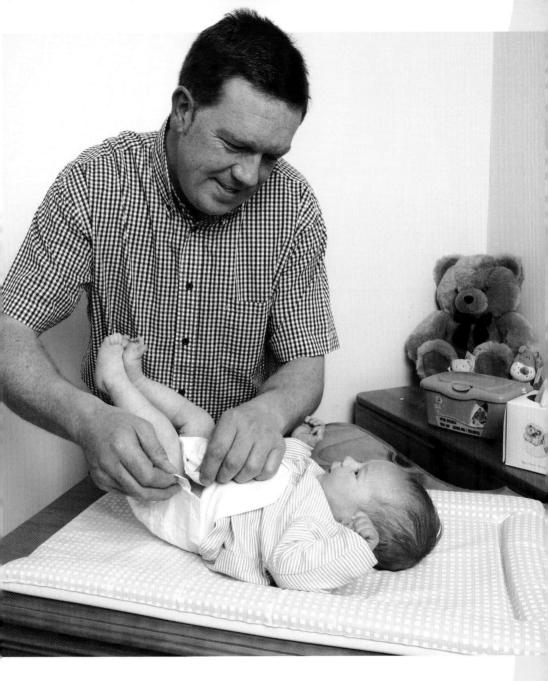

11

I made baby
noises.

When I was a
toddler, I sat in
a high chair.

15

16

I had to use a potty.

18

I pushed my baby walker.

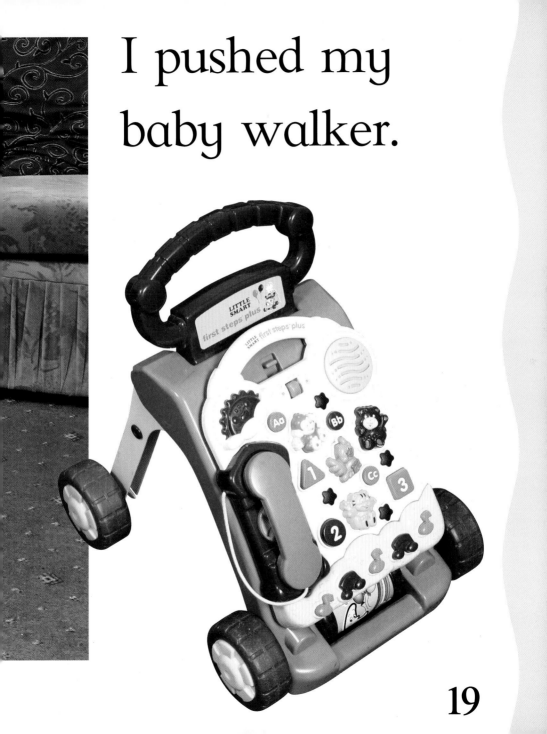

I learned lots of words.

Mama

21

I'm glad I'm a big boy now.

Word bank

Look back for these words and pictures.

Baby

Baby walker

Boy

High chair

Juice

Nappy

Play mat

Potty

Toddler